D0007181

HOW GOD MADE THE WORLD

This story has been extracted from
Read Aloud Bible Stories, Vol. 3
by Ella Lindvall

Printed in Mexico

MOODY PRESS

Do you like to make things?
God likes to make things.
It was God who made the world.

God said, "Come, light!"
And the dark ran away.
God said, "That's good."
He called the light DAY.
He called the dark NIGHT.

Then God said,
"Come, sky!"
and the sky came.
Next God said,

"Come, dry land!"
Up came the big hills.
Up came the little hills.
Down ran the water
into God's place for it.
God said, "That's good."
Then God said,

"Come, plants!"
Up grew the apple trees.
Up grew the corn.
Up grew the beans.
Up grew the green grass.
God said, "That's good."
Then He said,

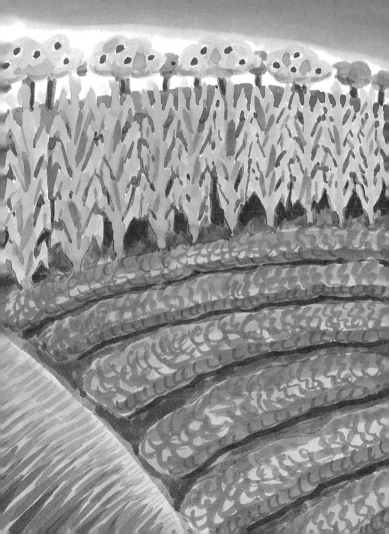

"Come, sun!
Come, moon!
Shine in the sky!"
(He made the stars too.)
God said, "That's good."
Then He said,

"Come, fish!
Come, birds!"
God made the big fish.
God made the little fish.
God made the big birds.
God made the little birds.
God said, "That's good."
Then He said,

"Come, animals!"
God made the cats.
God made the dogs.
God made the horses.
God made the lions.
God made the bears.

God made the bunnies.
God made the butterflies.
God made the wiggily worms.
God made them all.
Then He said,

"Now let's make PEOPLE!"
First, God made a daddy.
His name was Adam.

God brought His animals
to Adam.
Adam said, "Your name
will be dog.
And your name will be cat.
Your name will be horse.
Your name will be lion."
He gave a name
to every one.

Last of all,
God made a beautiful mommy.
God brought her to Adam.
And Adam was very pleased.
Adam said,
"Her name will be Eve."

Then God looked
at all He had made—
day and night,
sky and water,
land and plants,
sun and moon,
shiny stars,
fish and birds,
animals and
PEOPLE.

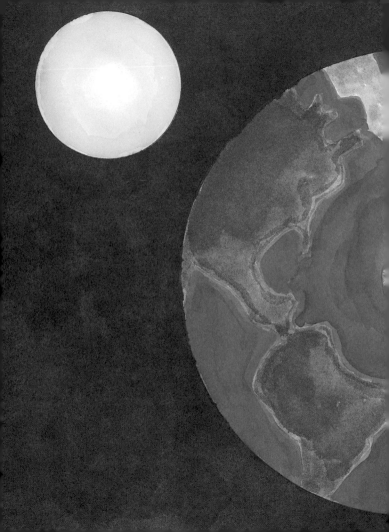

God was pleased
with everything.
God said,
"It's VERY good!"

What did you learn?

God did it.
It was God
who made everything.
And He made everything
JUST RIGHT.

About the Author

Ella K. Lindvall (A.B., Taylor University; Wheaton College; Northern Illinois University) is a mother and former elementary school teacher. She is the author of *The Bible Illustrated for Little Children,* and *Read-Aloud Bible Stories, volumes I, II, and III.*